MASTER LACROSSE FOR BEGINNERS

Your Step-by-Step Guide to Learning Lacrosse Fundamentals, Techniques, and Tips in an Easy and Beginner-Friendly Way

SHIRLEY G. ELSTON

CHAPTER ONE

INTRODUCTION

Lacrosse is a quick-moving, high-intensity sport that has become more and more well-liked all around the world. A little rubber ball is caught, carried, and passed using a stick in this team sport in order to score goals. Although girls' lacrosse is a more recent development and has seen tremendous growth in recent years, lacrosse has a long history. In this thorough guide, we'll look at the development and history of girls' lacrosse, go through the sport's fundamental concepts like goals and gameplay, evaluate the important gear needed for ladies, and look at how girls' teams should be positioned on the field.

The Development of Girls' Lacrosse:

Lacrosse has a long history that can be traced to Native American tribes in North America, especially those of the Haudenosaunee (Iroquois) people. Their societies placed a high value on the game, also known as "stickball" or "baggataway," which was used to resolve conflicts, prepare warriors, and show respect for the Creator.

In the 19th century, lacrosse gained popularity in Canada and the United States as it expanded outside of Indigenous communities. However, ladies' lacrosse did not develop until much later because it was predominantly a male-dominated sport at the time.

Girls' lacrosse has grown significantly during the 1920s and 1930s, when women's sports began to take off in the United States. females' lacrosse was first organized and promoted when physical education instructors and female athletes realized how important it was for females to have access to sports and athletic possibilities. Rosabelle Sinclair, a physical education teacher from Baltimore, Maryland, wrote the first set of regulations exclusively for women's lacrosse in 1933, which was a crucial turning point for girls' lacrosse. These regulations kept the spirit of the sport while adapting the game to account for the physical differences between men and women.

At the high school and collegiate levels, girls' lacrosse grew throughout the middle of the 20th century. Since its founding in 1931, the United States Women's Lacrosse Association (USWLA) has played a crucial role in developing and regulating the game for women. In order to create a single organization in charge of both men's and women's lacrosse, the USWLA joined with the men's regulatory body, the United States Lacrosse (US Lacrosse), in 2001.

Girls' lacrosse will be included in the Olympics in 2028, which will further its development and appeal. More girls are playing lacrosse at the youth level thanks to the increased interest in the sport spurred by the Olympics' global exposure.

Today, there are numerous nations playing girls' lacrosse, with the United States, Canada, Australia, and England ranking among the top players in the sport. It is still expanding, and efforts are still being made to reach new areas and communities.

GETTING THE BASICS RIGHT: GIRLS' LACROSSE GOALS, RULES, AND GAMEPLAY

Objectives:

To score more goals than the opposition is the primary goal in girls' lacrosse. A team achieves this by catching, carrying, and passing the ball with their lacrosse sticks, then shooting it into the opposing team's goal. At the conclusion of the game, the team with the most goals wins.

Rules:

Teams and players: There are 12 players on the field for a girls' lacrosse team, including the goalkeeper. A team's roster can have more players, allowing for substitutions during play. The ball is placed in the middle of the field between the sticks of two players to start the game, and they compete to get possession.

Stick and Ball: The pockets on girls' lacrosse sticks are shallower than those on boys' sticks. Better passing and ball control are made possible by this design. The ball is usually constructed of solid rubber and is yellow in color.

Girls' lacrosse is regarded as a non-contact sport. Contact rules. Aggressive checking and physical play are not allowed, however certain physical contact is allowed, such as stick checks and body positions.

The offside rule, which mandates that a specific number of players from each team stay on their defensive side of the field, is in effect in girls' lacrosse. Penalties apply for disregarding this rule.

Girls' lacrosse contains a variety of fouls, including slashing, tripping, and charging, which lead to penalties. Her side is shorthanded while the penalty is in effect as the guilty player must serve time in the penalty box. When the ball crosses the goal line and rebounds between the goalposts, the goal is scored. The value of each goal is one point.

Gameplay:

The game of girls' lacrosse is regarded for being fast-paced and exciting. The ball must be carried by players, passed to teammates, and shot into the goal of the other team using their sticks. The game necessitates continuous movement, planning, and cooperation. Players employ a variety of strategies, including cradling (a way to keep hold of the ball while sprinting), dodging (to elude defenders), and shooting (to score goals). In order to keep the other team from scoring, the goalie performs a crucial defensive role by stopping shots. Games usually have two halves, each lasting a certain period of time, and a halftime intermission. In some competitions, overtime sessions may be utilized to break ties. The winning team is the one with the most goals at the end of the contest.

NECESSARY PIECES OF GIRLS' LACROSSE EQUIPMENT

Specific equipment is needed for girls' lacrosse to ensure safety and proper gaming. The stick, goggles, and mouthguard are the three necessities for players.

Stick: The main device used to catch, carry, and pass the ball in lacrosse is the stick. The head and the shaft are the two basic components. The player's handle is provided by the shaft, while the head features a mesh pocket that holds the ball. Girls' lacrosse sticks feature a shallower pocket than boys' sticks, which encourages a quicker release of the ball and better ball control. Specific guidelines must be followed regarding the stick's length.

Lacrosse goggles are made to shield the player's eyes from any collisions from the ball or the sticks of opposing players. They should fit securely and pleasantly because they are made precisely to fit the curve of a woman's face.

Mouthguard: A mouthguard is essential for preventing dental and facial injuries in athletes. It is worn over the teeth and aids in shock absorption during active activity.

Gloves, cleats, and additional padding are available extras that provide further protection. Despite the fact that the game is deemed non-contact, wearing protective equipment is crucial to avoiding injuries that can arise from accidental contact

Girls' Teams' Lacrosse Field Setup and Positions:

Although lacrosse fields come in a variety of sizes, the specifications for girls' lacrosse fields follow guidelines established by the US Lacrosse and other regulating bodies. The rectangular area has distinct marks to indicate the boundaries of the several zones.

The Scene:

The goal area has a radius of 8.5 meters (15 yards) and surrounds the goal in a semicircle. Inside the goal area, only the goalkeeper and defensive players are permitted; offensive players must stay outside.

The defensive and attacking zones are separated by a line called the restraining line. Players must stay behind the restraining line throughout a draw until possession is established.

The 8-Meter Arc: This arc marks the perimeter for defenders during a free-position shot and is placed 8 meters from the goal. Attackers must stay outside the shot's arc at all times.

The draw occurs in the center of the field here at the start of the game, at the beginning of each half, and following a goal. The referee throws the ball into the air for the two players, one from each team, to contest ownership of it while holding their sticks horizontally above it.

Positions:

Players are often given distinct positions in girls' lacrosse according to their abilities and talents. While each team's roster may differ, the following are some typical positions in girls' lacrosse:

Goalkeeper (GK): As the final line of defense, the goalkeeper is essential in stopping goals. She also has knee pads, a chest protector, and a helmet with a face mask on her headgear.

Defenders work to stop the other team from scoring on defense (D). They must cooperate to form a powerful defense unit and utilize their sticks to check and block opponents.

Midfield (M): Midfielders switch between offense and defense while covering the full field. In addition to moving the ball and aiding the offense and defense, they are in charge of winning draws.

Attack (A): Attackers concentrate on exerting pressure on the opposing defense and scoring goals. They avoid opponents by moving quickly and using their stick abilities to set up scoring opportunities.

During breaks in play, substitutions are permitted, and coaches cleverly rotate their players to keep them fresh and able to respond to various game scenarios.

Conclusion:

Since its inception, girls' lacrosse has advanced significantly, evolving from a specialized sport to a vibrant, well-liked, and well-recognized pastime. The history of the sport, which is rooted in Indigenous customs, is proof of its cultural importance and enduring allure.

Players, coaches, and fans all benefit from having a foundational understanding of the fundamentals of girls' lacrosse, including its goals, regulations, and gameplay. The emphasis on non-contact play and the use of equipment designed specifically for female athletes make the activity safe and entertaining for the participants. More and more young athletes are embracing the athleticism, teamwork, and strategic elements of girls' lacrosse as the sport gains popularity throughout the world. Girls' lacrosse's involvement in the Olympics has given it a platform to be seen by a larger public, further driving its rise. Girls' lacrosse continues to be a thrilling and dynamic sport, grabbing the hearts of players and spectators alike with its distinctive combination of skill, speed, and sportsmanship. Future generations of athletes will definitely be inspired by the sport as it develops to pick up a lacrosse stick, hit the field, and make priceless experiences in the world of girls' lacrosse.

CHAPTER TWO

FUNDAMENTALS OF GIRLS' LACROSSE

It takes a variety of skills to play lacrosse, including stick holding, passing, shooting, and ground ball tactics. Lacrosse is an exciting and dynamic sport. In this thorough course, we'll go into the foundations of girls' lacrosse, emphasizing proper cradling, passing, and shooting methods for the stick. In order to improve accuracy and quick release, we'll also look at ground ball and scooping skills, as well as catching and throwing. Finally, we'll look at shooting tactics, such as overhand, sidearm, and underhand shots, which are crucial for female lacrosse players to master in order to excel on the field.

Techniques for Cradling, Passing, and Shooting While Handling a Lacrosse Stick

Cradling:

In girls' lacrosse, cradling is a crucial technique that entails holding onto the ball while moving or dodging defenders. Cradling's main objective is to stop the ball from slipping out of the lacrosse stick's pocket.

To cradle effectively, take the following actions:

a. Grip: Place your non-dominant hand on the shaft of the stick and your dominant hand closer to the head of the stick. Keep your fingers relaxed and avoid squeezing the object too tightly.

b. Wrist Movement: By rocking your wrists back and forth, you can make the lacrosse head sway. While you move, this motion maintains the ball firmly in the pocket.

c. Keep Your Eyes Up: As you cradle, keep your eyes up and on the field to stay vigilant for potential defenders and your surroundings.

Passing:

The fundamental skill of passing entails accurately and efficiently moving the ball to teammates. Maintaining possession and creating scoring opportunities require proper passing technique.

For a successful pass, you must:

a. Grip: For improved control and power, adopt the proper grip while holding the stick with your hands apart.

b. Rotate your hips and shoulders in the direction of the target to increase the force of the pass.

c. Follow Through: To keep your precision and control after releasing the ball, follow through with your stick.

d. To make sure your teammates are prepared to receive the pass, communicate with them.

Shooting Methods:

Shooting is the ability that enables players to score goals, which is a crucial component in girls' lacrosse. The overhand, sidearm, and underhand shots are just a few of the several shooting tactics.

a. The most popular shooting method in girls' lacrosse is the overhand shot. How to make an overhand shot:

i. Set up your stance with your body facing the goal and your feet shoulder-width apart.

ii. Bring your stick slightly behind your head as you cradle the ball.

iii. Step forward with your non-dominant foot as you shot to shift your weight to the front foot.

iv. Swing your wrists forward and release the ball overhand in the direction of the goal.

b. When shooting in close range or around defenders, the sidearm shot is employed. How to fire a sidearm shot:

i. Assume a shooting position by slanting your body toward the target.

ii. Keep your stick parallel to the ground as you cradle the ball.

iii. Extend your dominant arm while rotating your hips and shoulders forward.

iv. Release the ball with a sidearm motion toward the goal by snapping your wrists forward.

c. Underhand Shot: When shooting from a close distance or when a goalie is challenging your overhand shot, you should use the underhand shot. How to make an underhand shot:

i. Put your feet shoulder-width apart and turn your body toward the goal.

ii. Hold the ball while lowering your stick to your waist.

iii. With your front foot, advance while shifting your weight.

iv. As you raise your wrists, underhand throw the ball in the direction of the goal.

Ground Ball and Scooping Techniques

Ground balls occur when the ball is on the ground and several players from both teams try to scoop it up and take possession. Maintaining possession, switching from defense to offense, and creating scoring opportunities all depend on winning ground balls.

To scoop a ground ball effectively:

The ball should be approached with confidence and urgency. Keep an eye on the ball and predict where it will go.

Low Center of Gravity: To create a solid foundation, crouch down with your knees bent. You can stay balanced and respond swiftly because of this.

Scoop the Ball: When you get to the ball, use the head's bottom edge to scoop it into the pocket with your lacrosse stick. To ensure you don't miss the ball, keep your stick close to the ground.

Securing the Ball: After scooping it up, place it in your stick's pocket and shield it from defenders with your body and stick. Accuracy and quick release development for catching and throwing:

In girls' lacrosse, catching and throwing are fundamental abilities that help players keep possession of the ball, move it, and set up scoring possibilities. For successful games, developing rapid release and precision in catching and throwing is crucial.

Catching:

Effective baseball catching requires:

a. Hand Position: Spread your hands out on the stick to create a broad pocket to safely capture the ball.

b. Maintain eye contact as you follow the ball into the stick's pocket.

c. Give with the catch by letting your hands and elbows relax in order to absorb the impact of the ball.

d. After catching the ball, transfer it rapidly to a more advantageous location for passing or shooting.

Throwing:

It's essential to practice accurate and rapid throws if you want to keep possession of the ball and distribute it wisely.

a. Grip: For improved control and accuracy, hold the stick with your hands apart.

b. To produce power and accuracy, rotate your shoulders and hips in the direction of the target.

c. Follow Through: To improve accuracy after releasing the ball, continue to throw with your stick while directing it in the intended direction.

d. Quick Release: After catching the ball, release it immediately to increase your speed and effectiveness.

Shooting Methods: Overhand, Sidearm, and Underhand Shots

One of the most thrilling components of girls' lacrosse is shooting since it gives players the chance to score goals and greatly improve their team's performance. A player's offensive skills are improved by becoming proficient in a variety of shooting tactics, including the overhand, sidearm, and underhand shots.

Overhand Slugger:

Girls' lacrosse players most frequently use the overhand shot, which offers precision and power when shooting from a distance. How to make an overhand shot:

a. Shooting Stance: Place your feet shoulder-width apart and lean sideways toward the target.

b. Cradle: As you get ready to shoot, cradle the ball with both hands while holding the stick.

c. Bring the stick a little bit behind your head as you shift your weight to your rear foot.

d. Step forward with your front foot while snapping your wrists in front of you to release the ball overhand.

e. Follow Through: To increase accuracy, allow your stick to continue moving after you release it.

Arms-side shot:

When attempting to score or avoid defenders, the sidearm shot is the best option. How to fire a sidearm shot:

Shooting Stance: Stand with your feet shoulder-width apart, your body facing the goal.

b. Cradle: As you get ready to shoot, hold the stick with both hands parallel to the ground while cradling the ball.

c. Weight Transfer: Shift your weight to your front foot while rotating your hips and shoulders forward.

d. Release the ball with a sidearm motion toward the goal by snapping your wrists forward.

e. For accuracy and power, follow through with your stick in the intended direction after releasing the shot.

Unhandled Shot:

When facing a hostile goaltender or shooting from a close distance, the underhand shot is quite helpful. How to make an underhand shot:

a. Shooting Stance: Stand with your feet shoulder-width apart, your body facing the goal.

b. Cradle: Place the ball in your lap while lowering the stick to your waist.

c. Weight Transfer: Step forward while shifting your weight to your front foot.

d. Release the ball with an underhand motion toward the goal while snapping your wrists upward.

e. Follow Through: To increase accuracy, let your stick follow through in the direction of the shot.

To become confident and skilled in using these shooting tactics during game scenarios, it is imperative to consistently practice them.

Conclusion:

Girls' lacrosse fundamentals establish the foundation for athletes to succeed on the field by equipping them with the required abilities to control the lacrosse stick deftly, pass precisely, shoot precisely, and secure possession with ground balls and scooping techniques.

For players to contribute to the success of their team and take pleasure in the fast-paced and dynamic nature of the sport, they must master these key abilities. The fundamentals of offensive play are cradling, passing, and shooting methods, which enable players to keep control of the ball, pass it to teammates, and create scoring opportunities. Effective execution of these skills requires the right body alignment, wrist movement, and hand placement. Techniques involving the ground ball and scooping are crucial for controlling the ball, switching from defense to offensive, and winning battles for possession. In order to scoop the ball off the ground successfully during game scenarios, proper body placement, footwork, and stick technique are essential. Throwing and catching are essential techniques for moving the ball and keeping possession. Accuracy and a quick release in catching and throwing must be developed if you want to move the ball effectively and execute good offensive plays.

Players can score goals and make a substantial contribution to the success of their team by using shooting styles including the overhand, sidearm, and underhand shots. To become effective at using them from various spots on the field, players must practice these varied shooting tactics. Overall, constant practice, determination, and a desire to develop one's skills are necessary to learn the foundations of girls' lacrosse. Players will acquire confidence in their skills as they advance in their lacrosse careers, obtain a better grasp of the sport, and add to the excitement and competition of girls' lacrosse at all levels. Players may completely enjoy the excitement and camaraderie that girls' lacrosse offers by embracing the principles and continually improving their skills.

CHAPTER THREE

GIRLS' LACROSSE OFFENSE PLAY

Girls' lacrosse's offense is essential because it enables teams to generate scoring opportunities and score goals. Understanding offensive formations, the functions of attacker positions, the adaptability of midfielders, and crucial evading tactics are necessary for an attacking plan to be successful. We will examine the nuances of playing offense in girls' lacrosse in this complete tutorial, concentrating on offensive formations, attacker positions, midfielder duties, and various dodging maneuvers including the split dodge, roll dodge, and face dodge.

Understanding the Fundamentals of Offensive Formations for Girls' Teams

Teams in girls' lacrosse use a variety of attacking formations to increase their chances of scoring and adjust to changing game circumstances. Player positioning and ball movement are dictated by offensive formations, opening up opportunities to take advantage of defensive deficiencies. In girls' lacrosse, the following offensive formations are frequently used:

Formation 3-3:

One of the most popular offensive formations in girls' lacrosse is the 3-3. It calls for three attackers to be placed in the crease or close to the goal as well as three attackers to be placed outside the goal. The goal is to generate movement and passing lanes in order to disorient the opposition and locate open shooting possibilities.

The three attackers who are closest to the crease are known as "creasers" and are in charge of setting up scoring opportunities from close range. They need to be skilled at ducking, shooting in confined locations, and using rapid stick skills.

Attackers on the perimeter: The three assailants set up shop around the 12-meter fan. Their job is to move the ball swiftly, hold onto it, and look for chances to feed crease attackers or shoot uncontested from the outside.

Formation: 2-3-1

Another common attacking formation is the 2-3-1, which offers a balanced approach with two attackers up top, three in the middle, and one in the crease.

Top Attackers: The top two attackers are in charge of starting offensive plays, dodging, and generating scoring opportunities for themselves or their teammates.

Midfielders: The three midfielders serve a dual function as transition players and scoring threats. They are situated between the top attackers and the crease attacker. They need to be flexible offensive players who can support both offense and defense.

One crease attacker is responsible for creating scoring opportunities near the goal. Excellent placement, stick handling, and the capacity to complete in confined spaces are requirements for this position.

Motion Infraction:

A fluid offensive tactic known as "motion offense" places an emphasis on player cuts, ball rotation, and constant movement. Motion offense, as opposed to set formations, depends on players reading the opposition, making cuts, and creating opportunities based on the dynamics of the game.

Movement: Players frequently shift positions, cut, and move around, making it difficult for the defense to maintain coverage and anticipate offensive moves.

Ball Movement: Players quickly switch possession of the ball among themselves, preventing the defense from settling into a convenient position.

Cuts and Picks: Players make deliberate cuts toward the net or use picks, which involve obstructing opponents to make room for teammates to pass or shoot.

Scoring and Assisting Goals for Attackers

Given that they are generally in charge of scoring goals and providing assists for their teammates, the attackers are essential to the offensive plan. There are particular attacker positions, each with distinct duties:

A first house

The attacker who is positioned behind the goal is referred to as "X," or the First Home. This player serves as the offense's quarterback, calling plays and starting offensive actions.

The First Home's responsibilities include having superior vision and a high lacrosse IQ. Setting up attacking plays, supplying cutters, and producing scoring opportunities from beyond the goal are their responsibilities.

A second house

The First Home is situated on one side, while the Second Home, also called the "wing," is on the opposite side. They collaborate with the First Home to design offensive plays and take advantage of scoring chances.

The Second Home's duties include being adept at cutting and reading defenses to spot openings for shots or passes.

A third house

The Third Home, also referred to as the "crease attacker," is positioned close to the crease and frequently the player in charge of converting close-range scoring opportunities.

The Third Home's responsibilities include finishing in small areas and having quick hands and strong stick abilities. Quick feeds from the First Home or Second Home are frequently used by them to score.

Midfielders: Scoring Threats and Transition Players

Players who are capable of playing both offense and defense are midfielders.

They are essential in transition, swiftly transferring the ball from defense to offense, and they also help create scoring opportunities. Different types of midfielders include:

Attacking midfielders

The primary goals of offensive midfielders are to create scoring opportunities and offensive plays.

In order to breach the defense, make space, and set up scoring opportunities, offensive midfielders have a variety of responsibilities. Additionally, they must be able to shoot accurately from outside the paint.

Midfielders who play defense:

Defense-to-offense transitions and defensive support are the main areas of concentration for defensive midfielders. Defensive midfielders' responsibilities include clearing the ball from the defensive end and helping to ground balls. By getting the ball to the attackers fast, they also help the team's transition game.

Dual-Position Midfielders:

Two-way midfielders are midfielders who perform well in both offensive and defensive situations.

Two-way midfielders are important members of the team because they can easily switch from defense to offensive and assist in many different areas of the game.

Techniques for Dodging: Split Dodging, Roll Dodging, and Face Dodging for Girls

A player's ability to dodge is a crucial offensive skill that enables them to slip past defenders and open up scoring chances. There are various efficient dodging strategies used in girls' lacrosse, such as the split dodge, roll dodge, and face dodge.

Double Dodge:

One of the most popular and successful evading strategies in girls' lacrosse is the split dodge. To change direction and avoid the defender's check, it involves separating their body.

Implementation: To execute a split dodge:
a. With your dominant hand, begin by cradling the ball.

b. As you approach the defender, shield the ball with your non-dominant shoulder.

c. Quickly step forward with your non-dominant foot as the opponent tries to check you, then push off with your dominant foot in the opposite direction.

d. To shield the ball from the defender, switch your cradle to the opposite hand.

e. accelerate in the new direction as you move away from the defender.

Dodge Roll:

By rolling your body away from the defender's check, you can dodge defenders and change directions quickly. Implementation: To execute a roll dodge:

a. With your dominant hand, begin by cradling the ball.

b. Use your non-dominant shoulder to shield the ball as you approach the defender.

c. In order to turn your body away from the defender, plant your non-dominant foot.

d. Roll your body away from the defender's check while switching your cradle to the other hand.

e. accelerate in the new direction as you move away from the defender.
Face Off:

The face dodge is a sneaky evading move that is used to quickly change from one direction to the other.
Implementation: To execute a face dodge:

a. With your dominant hand, begin by cradling the ball.

b. Fake as though you're going to dodge in one direction as you get closer to the defender, like to your left.

c. Move the cradle and your body weight swiftly to the other side, such as your right.

d. To shield the ball from the defender's check, use your free hand.

e. Take advantage of the space the false provided by accelerating away from the defender in the new direction.

Attackers and midfielders can use dodging as a crucial attacking talent to get ahead of defenders, advance toward goal, and start scoring chances. By mastering these dodging methods, players can increase their offensive flexibility and unpredictability, making it harder for defenders to properly cover them.

Conclusion:
In girls' lacrosse, playing offense calls for a blend of tactical knowledge, technical proficiency, and the capacity for teamwork. Teams can take advantage of defensive deficiencies and create scoring opportunities by utilizing the structure provided by offensive formations for player positioning and ball movement. Attackers are essential to offensive, with certain positions like First Home, Second Home, and Third Home each having distinct duties in goal-scoring and goal-assistance.

Midfielders are skilled athletes who can assist on both offense and defense, and they are essential in the changeover from defense to offense. While defensive midfielders concentrate on assisting the defense and passing the ball, offensive midfielders excel at creating scoring opportunities. A balanced approach is provided by two-way midfielders, who are excellent in both the offensive and defensive facets of the game.

Players need offensive talents that allow them to get past defenders and create scoring opportunities, such as the split dodge, roll dodge, and face dodge. By mastering these dodges, a player's offensive game gains a degree of unpredictability that makes them more challenging to defend.

Girls' lacrosse players that thrive offensively must consistently improve their abilities, communication, and comprehension of offensive concepts.

For the purpose of dismantling defensive fortifications and generating high-probability scoring opportunities, efficient ball movement, player cuts, and offensive positioning are essential.

In order to be effective, an offensive plan in girls' lacrosse must strike a balance between individual talent, group effort, and tactical application. Players and teams can improve their offensive performance and develop into fierce competitors on the lacrosse field by embracing the complexities of offensive formations, attacker positions, midfielder duties, and dodging skills.

CHAPTER FOUR

DEFENSE POSITIONS IN GIRLS LACROSSE

The goal of defense in girls' lacrosse is to keep the other team from scoring and regaining possession of the ball. Strategic consideration, interpersonal interaction, and individual defensive expertise are necessary for effective defensive play. This in-depth manual will examine the nuances of playing defense in girls' lacrosse, emphasizing defensive formations and techniques, guarding the crease, the roles of close defense players, and team defense strategies, such as sliding and double-teaming.

Girls' Team Defensive Strategies and Formations:

Teams in girls' lacrosse use a variety of defensive formations and methods to thwart the attacking plays of the opposition and force errors. In order to maintain the best possible defensive coverage and pressure, defensive formations determine player placement and movements. Here are some typical defensive tactics and lacrosse formations for girls:

Man-to-Man Protection:
Using the simple defensive tactic of man-to-man defense, each defender is tasked

with containing a certain offensive player. The main objective is to prevent the offensive player from receiving passes, advancing to the goal, or shooting.

Man-to-man defense relies on effective communication to make sure that defenders replace players when appropriate and prevent leaving offensive players unmarked.

Coverage: Defenders must remain close to the offensive players they have been assigned to, limiting passing paths and shooting angles with their sticks and bodies.

Recovery: It's critical for other defenders to slide and offer support if an offensive player succeeds to get past her defender in order to stop an uncontested shot.

Area Defense:

Instead of focusing on tagging specific players, zone defense entails defenders covering predetermined sections of the field. The main goal is to put up defensive barriers, block passing lanes, and make the attack commit errors.

Defenders cooperate to protect particular zones, such as the perimeter, passing routes, or the crucial scoring area in front of the goal (the crease).

Zone defense relies heavily on communication to ensure that defenders rotate and adjust their positions in order to maintain coverage.

Zone defense depends on the offense's ability to move the ball well to locate holes and exploit defensive weaknesses. To maintain efficient zone coverage, defenders must anticipate the ball's movement.

Defensive formations, like the rotating zone, flat defense, or diamond defense, can be changed to accommodate a team's strengths, an opponent's playing style, and game circumstances. In order for players to effectively execute the defensive plan during games, coaches work with them to ensure that they understand their duties within it.

Protecting the Crease and Interacting with the Goalie

In girls' lacrosse, protecting the crease is essential because there is where the other team looks to set up scoring opportunities. To effectively defend the crease, the goalkeeper and defenders must cooperate. Key components of guarding the crease include:

Positioning: To create a defensive wall and deny the offensive players access to the goal, defenders must maintain correct positioning around the crease.

Defenders should keep their bodies in a low defensive position and remain in between their attacking player and the goal.

Defenders should be prepared to rapidly slide to assist a teammate in stopping an offensive player who is attempting to drive toward the goal.

Double-teaming: Defenders may use double-teaming strategies to increase pressure on an attacking player near the crease who is talented.

Interaction with the goalie:

Effective defensive play requires communication with the goalie. Defenders are required to promptly and clearly communicate the location of attacking players and any possible dangers.

Calling Out Players: As offensive players approach the crease or receive the ball, defenders should yell out their names or positions.

Defensemen should communicate shot attempts and shooting locations to the goalie so that they can get ready to make saves.

goaltender as Communicator: The goaltender should also alert the defenders of the movements and positions of the offensive players.

Marking and forcing opponents is a close defense player's specialty.

Close defense players are defenders tasked with containing the attackers of the other side as they approach the goal. Their main objective is to keep the offensive players from getting advantageous positions and shooting unopposed. The following are crucial elements of close defense:

Close defensive players must tightly mark the offensive players they are assigned to, limiting their movement with their sticks and body placement.

A close defense player should take up a position between their offensive player and the goal while remaining "goal-side" to deter attackers from approaching the goal.

Stick Checks: To stop an offensive player from cradling or passing the ball, close defense players may execute controlled stick checks.

Force: To move the offensive player away from the goal and into less dangerous positions, close defense players must exert the proper pressure on them.

Stick Position: To prevent an offensive player from attempting a pass or shot, close defense players should place their sticks in the passing paths and shooting lanes.

Body Position: Close defensive players can obstruct an offensive player's advancement and prevent them from driving to the goal by keeping good body placement and staying low.

Double-teaming: In specific circumstances, close defense players may work with teammates to perform a double team on an offensive player with skill, applying more pressure to her and inducing errors.

Sliding and double-teaming: Girls' Team Defense Techniques

Essential team defense strategies like sliding and double-teaming call for effective communication and well-coordinated defense work. Defenders can support one another and reduce scoring opportunities for the offensive team by using these strategies. In girls' lacrosse, sliding and double-teaming operate as follows:

Sliding:

Sliding is when a defender moves away from the player she is tasked with defending to assist a teammate who is defending an offensive player who is trying to drive for the goal. The ball carrier must be put under immediate pressure by the sliding defender in order to stop her aggressive move.

The offensive player must not pass the ball before the slide arrives, hence it is important that slides are timed correctly. To let her teammate know when to expect support, the defender who starts the slide should let her teammate know what she plans to do.

Recovery: To create a smooth defensive rotation after the sliding defender has pressured the ball carrier, the initial defender must rapidly recover to mark another attacking player.

Double-Teaming:

Double-teaming is a strategy in which two defenders cooperate to apply pressure to one offensive player in particular, causing her to act hastily or turn the ball over.

To stop the attacking player from escaping the pressure, defenders must coordinate their double-team and communicate with one other. In order to induce a turnover, the double-team must either force a poor pass or knock the ball off the offensive player's stick. Double-teaming can be beneficial, but defenders must employ it wisely and make sure no offensive players are left unmarked.

Strong interpersonal relationships, mutual trust, and teamwork are essential components of team defense. In order to sabotage the offensive team's plays and force turnovers, players must cooperate, understand their duties in sliding and double-teaming, and work together.

Conclusion

Girls' lacrosse defense is a complex and dynamic component of the game that calls for a blend of specialized defensive abilities, smart thinking, and efficient teamwork. Man-to-man defense and zone defense, for example, specify player placement and ball movement to counter the offensive plays of the opposing side. As the area around the goal is where the opposition side attempts to create scoring opportunities, defending the crease is a crucial duty for defenders. In order to preserve the crease, close defensive players are essential for marking and shoving opponents away from the goal. They also work well with the goalie to coordinate their efforts.

Team defense strategies like sliding and double-teaming are employed to aid one another and reduce the offensive team's scoring potential. While double-teaming seeks to create turnovers by applying additional pressure to a single offensive player, effective sliding entails timely and coordinated efforts to pressure the ball carrier. Players must constantly improve their unique defensive techniques, including as body placement, stick checks, and footwork, to excel on defense. In order to coordinate attempts to thwart the offensive moves and ensure flawless defensive rotations, they must also properly communicate with their teammates.

Here are some extra defense-related advice and suggestions for girls' lacrosse:

Winning ground ball battles is crucial in girls' lacrosse because it gives the defensive team possession and stops the offensive team from taking advantage of opportunities. In ground ball battles, players must be forceful and aggressive in order to scoop the ball and gain possession for their team.

Defensive Footwork: Defenders who want to remain agile and balanced while marking their opponents must have good footwork. Effective defensive footwork enables players to cover gaps, retain their defensive positions, and respond quickly to offensive moves.

Communication between teammates and foresight into the opponent's moves are essential for effective defense. To enable the team to react quickly, defenders must convey attacking player movements, potential threats, and sliding opportunities.

Stick checks are an effective defensive tactic, but players must use them carefully and under control to prevent consequences. Without using force or engaging in risky play, well-timed and performed stick checks can interfere with the opponent's stick handling and passing.

Defenders must have patience and control to prevent unwarranted penalties or fouls that can give the opposition an edge. Successful defensive play requires the ability to remain calm under pressure and to follow defensive plans of action.

Transition Defense: In girls' lacrosse, switching from offense to defense (and vice versa) is essential. To provide proper defensive coverage and stop the opposition side from making quick breakouts, defenders must be aware of their placement during transitions.

Video analysis: Reviewing game tape and assessing defensive performances can give players and coaches important information. Players can identify their areas for growth, learn from their errors, and hone their defensive techniques with the help of video analysis.

Mental toughness: Playing defense can be both physically and mentally taxing, particularly during critical game situations. To withstand offensive pressure and keep the defense together, you must develop mental toughness and retain your attention on your defensive duties.

Teamwork and Support: Defense is a group activity that calls for cooperation among all defenders. Building a solid defensive base requires teammates to trust one another, support one another, and communicate clearly.

Continuous Learning: In girls' lacrosse, offensive moves and defensive tactics are always changing. Players and coaches should keep up with the most recent tactics and trends by attending clinics, consulting with coaches, and applying new defensive systems to improve their defensive abilities.

Finally, it should be noted that in girls' lacrosse, playing defense is a complex component of the game that necessitates a blend of individual abilities, strategic thinking, communication, and collaboration. Teams can modify their defensive strategy based on the playing style and strengths of the opposition using defensive formations and techniques like man-to-man defense and zone defense. To defend the crease and safeguard the goal, defenders must cooperate with the goalie and effectively communicate with him or her.

While slide and double-teaming are efficient team defense strategies used to help one another and thwart the other team's attacking moves, close defense players play a crucial part in marking and forcing opponents. Players can become formidable defenders and dramatically boost their team's success in girls' lacrosse by consistently honing their individual defensive talents, comprehending defensive methods, and engaging in efficient communication.

THANK YOU

Made in the USA
Middletown, DE
20 October 2023

41159151R00050